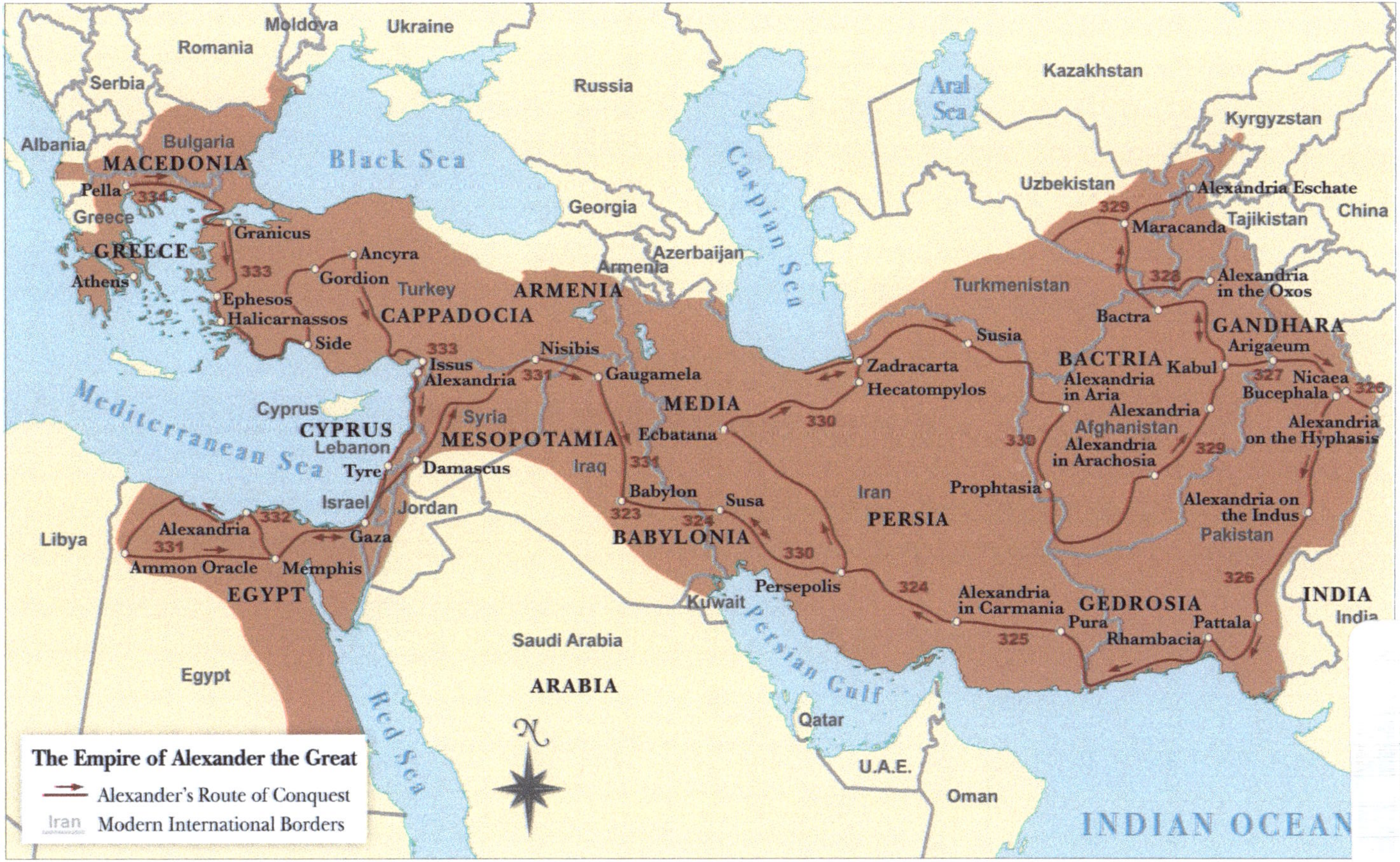
The Empire of Alexander the Great
Alexander's Route of Conquest
Iran Modern International Borders
MACEDONIA
GREECE
Pella
Athens
Granicus
Ephesos
Halicarnassos
Side
Ancyra
Gordion
CAPPADOCIA
ARMENIA
Issus
Alexandria
Nisibis
Gaugamela
MEDIA
MESOPOTAMIA
Ecbatana
Babylon
Susa
BABYLONIA
Persepolis
PERSIA
Zadracarta
Hecatompylos
Susia
Prophtasia
Alexandria in Carmania
GEDROSIA
Pura
Rhambacia
Pattala
Alexandria on the Indus
Alexandria on the Hyphasis
Nicaea
Bucephala
Arigaeum
GANDHARA
Kabul
BACTRIA
Bactra
Alexandria in Aria
Alexandria
Alexandria in Arachosia
Maracanda
Alexandria Eschate
Alexandria in the Oxos
INDIA
CYPRUS
Tyre
Damascus
Gaza
Alexandria
Memphis
Ammon Oracle
EGYPT
ARABIA
Black Sea
Caspian Sea
Aral Sea
Mediterranean Sea
Red Sea
Persian Gulf
INDIAN OCEAN
Albania
Serbia
Romania
Moldova
Ukraine
Bulgaria
Greece
Turkey
Russia
Georgia
Armenia
Azerbaijan
Cyprus
Lebanon
Syria
Israel
Jordan
Iraq
Kuwait
Saudi Arabia
Qatar
U.A.E.
Oman
Iran
Turkmenistan
Uzbekistan
Kazakhstan
Kyrgyzstan
Tajikistan
China
Afghanistan
Pakistan
India
Libya
Egypt
334
333
333
331
331
331
332
330
330
330
330
329
329
328
327
326
326
325
324
324
323

Other Books of Interest from Marquette Books

Former Congressman George R. Nethercutt Jr., Saving Patriotism: American Patriotism in a Global Era (2022). ISBN: 978-1-17327197-5-0

David Demers, The Killing of Bere Baudin: A Dystopian Novel (Book One of the Luminar Series, 2022). ISBNs: 978-1-17327197-8-1 (paperback) and 978-1-17327197-7-4 (e-book)

David Demers, Adventures of a Quixotic Professor: How One Man's Lifelong Passion for Social Justice Bristles Bureaucracies and Sparks a Landmark Free Speech Ruling (2021). ISBN: 978-1-7327197-9-8

Gary Bonvillian (ed.), The Savvy Investor's Guide for Doing Business in China (2019). ISBN: 978-1-17327197-0-5

Taehyun Kim, Daniel Erickson, and David Demers, How the Mass Media Really Work: An Introduction to Their Role as Institutions of Control and Change (2014). ISBN: 978-0-9833476-9-9

John Wheeler, Last Man Out: Memoirs of the Last Associated Press Reporter Castro Kicked Out of Cuba in the 1960s (2009, Demers Books). ISBN: 978-0-9816002-0-8

Hazel Dicken-Garcia and Giovanna Dell'Orto, Hated Ideas and the American Civil War Press (2008). ISBNs: 978-0-922993-88-8 (paperback) and 978-0-922993-89-5 (cloth)

ALEXANDER THE GREAT:
A Lyrical Biography

CHRISTINE O'BRIEN
JOHN MAXWELL O'BRIEN

MARQUETTE BOOKS
Phoenix, Arizona

Copyright © 2022 Christine O'Brien
and John Maxwell O'Brien

All rights reserved.
No part of this publication may be
reproduced, stored in a retrieval system, or
transmitted in any form or by any means,
electronic, mechanical, photo-copying, microfilming,
recording, or otherwise, without permission of
Marquette Books or the authors.

LIBRARY OF CONGRESS CONTROL NUMBER
2021953111

ISBN for this print edition: 978-1-7327197-4-3
ISBN for the electronic edition: 978-1-7327197-3-6

Distributed by Ingram Book Company
Cover illustration and interior design by Marquette Books
Edited and proofed by Liz Prouty

Page 1 map copyright © Peter Hermes Furian,
altered to include 2022 national borders by
Mapping Specialists, Ltd., Fitchburg, WI

The foreign language translations on the back cover are, from
top to bottom: Tamil, French, German, Gaelic, Arabic and Hindu

Published by

MARQUETTE BOOKS LLC
16421 North 31st Avenue
Phoenix, Arizona 85053
509-290-9240 (voice and text)
books@marquettebooks.com
https://MarquetteBooks.com

Contents

Introduction 7

I — A Royal Son is Born 9

II — Coming of Age 25

III — A Heroic King 45

IV — The Transformation 64

V — The Ambivalent Victor 68

VI — India 103

VII — Death in Babylon 112

A Select Bibliography 123

Table of Dates 124

Endnotes 126

About the Authors 128

For

Professor Paul Breines of Boston College, whose inspiration and dedication to teaching blossomed into the epic poem that follows.

Introduction

By the time of his death in Babylon on June 10, 323 BC, Alexander the Great had conquered more than two million square miles and was only thirty-two years of age.

He was an intrepid Macedonian warrior, superb strategist and masterful diplomat. He accepted and respected other peoples' cultures, treated women with dignity, and was exceptionally considerate of the disabled. He loved animals, large and small, domesticated and wild. His legacy is felt all over the world.

This slim volume serves as an introduction to Alexander, hoping to whet your appetite and lure you into a more extensive and deeper investigation of the questions that still resonate from his meteoric rise and mysterious demise. What follows is a lyrical biography — the first poem since the nineteenth century covering his life from birth to death. The poem is simple and unadorned, readable and rooted in historical research. It was written for curious teenagers as well as lifelong learners.

This biography also is illuminated with 48 paintings, drawings, sculptures, maps, and coins — masterpieces created through the ages by artists and historians. They are exquisite and depict Alexander and those close to him as well as many celebrated milestones of his career. A short list of notes associated mainly with the characters introduced in the poem is included at the end of the poem and is categorized by the numbers associated with the stanzas. A selective bibliography also follows the poem for those who are inspired to learn more.

    The authors are profoundly indebted to Laurel Hicks, Kathryn Ann Hill, Bill O'Brien, Dorothy O'Brien, and Lillian O'Brien for their outstanding suggestions in regard to the poem. Liz Prouty did a marvelous job of editing and proofing the manuscript. We are most grateful to Kathleen Zuris, our typist. We are also deeply indebted to Doug Jamieson for granting us permission to include several of his masterful drawings in this book.

Christine O'Brien
John Maxwell O'Brien
Spring 2022

Part I — A Royal Son Is Born

T wenty days into July
Three fifty-six BC
A boy of royal blood was birthed
Unto history

2

His father's name was Philip
Reigning King of Macedon
His mother was Olympias
And he her only son

3

The seers prophesied this child
To be a great commander
Superlatives were always used
Describing Alexander

The birth of Alexander as depicted in a 15th-century miniature (Musée de Petit Palais).

4

Less than average height he stood
One brown eye the other blue
But all that was foreseen for him
Was destined to ring true

5

In our histories we have
But fifty who are "Great"
And being first upon this list
Was Alexander's fate

6

And so I beckon to my Muse
Please whisper in my ear
A melic tale of peerlessness
I've yearned so long to hear

7

His life was filled with struggle
Almost from the very start
His parents ever colorful
Were culpable in part

8

More blessed with name and privilege
Than any child could be
He felt the pressures early on
Of meritocracy

9

His mother was a brilliant soul
Who came from royalty
Bringing him his greatest gift
Eternal loyalty

10

Tough as any man
Walking on this earth
Olympias was his sentinel
From the moment of his birth

Olympias and Alexander as depicted by Doug Jamieson
(copyrighted; used with permission)

11

A devotee of Bacchus
She entwined herself with snakes
Enough to ward off enemies
For both of their sakes

12

Descended from Achilles
Greatest hero of the Greeks
Expecting no less of her son
In laurels that he seeks

13

When he left for Asia
She said without demur
Be worthy of divine heritage
About which you can be sure

14

His father was a warrior
And thus not often home
All across his conquered lands
The king would often roam

15

Philip's plan was first to quell
The Greeks and those up north
Reluctantly most states succumbed
A Hellenic League sprang forth

16

This league was just a power tool
To keep the Greeks at bay
With everything at home secured
He'd need no longer stay

17

For Philip had a glorious dream
To conquer Asia Minor
Greece was a sweet victory
But Asia even finer

18

Little Alexander knew
The victories of his dad
But Philip's countless triumphs
Rarely made him glad

19

If all Alexander wanted
Was the power without merit
All he had to do was wait
And soon he would inherit

20

But this was just the problem
In Alexander's eyes
To him a soul without a dream
Inevitably dies

21

What more was there to wish for
What would be left to do
If Philip conquered everything
And left no conquests new

Philip II and Alexander as depicted by Doug Jamieson (copyrighted; used with permission)

22

It's been said that Fortune
Governs most of what we do
The other half or thereabouts
Is solely ruled by you

23

For Philip never made it
To the land he longed to see
But all his preparations
Helped his son, ironically

24

Indeed it has been argued
That without his father's aid
Foundations for world conquest
Would never have been laid

25

Philip gave him infantry
His crack corps was elite
Judged the best in ancient times
These men were hard to beat

26

The Royal Corps of Pages
Under Philip's keen direction
Gave him officer cadets
While thwarting insurrection

27

Technically a training post
For boys with a good name
They also served as hostages
To keep their fathers tame

28

The barons they were happy
That their sons had gained prestige
Another royal problem solved
With perspicacious ease

29

Philip became Archon
Over all of Thessaly
Paving Alexander's way
To secure that legacy

30

The gateway to the rest of Greece
Thessaly was quite a catch
An ally in the wars to come
Their cavalry was hard to match

31

One day a Thessalian
Had a superb horse to sell
He showed it to King Philip
But the horse did not act well

32

Although the finest ox-head brand
Of all the steeds in Greece
Bucephalus was a restless sort
And never seemed at peace

An ivory carving of Philip II from the 4th century BC (Archaeological Museum, Thessalonike)

33

Whenever someone tried to mount
Or just approach the beast
The animal would buck and rear
Until attempts had ceased

34

He forthwith ordered horse and keeper
Both to go away
Until that is he chanced to hear
What Alexander had to say

35

"What a horse they're losing
Cause they just can't handle it
No one even dares to try
How easily they quit"

36

At first King Philip chose
To ignore his son's remarks
But the boy persisted
And then there were some sparks

37

A goaded father asked his son
If you are such a wiz
Why not put some money
Where that mouth of yours is

38

The boy replied of course he would
And hoped it would suffice
To pay his father if he lost
The horse's asking price

39

Observers who were there
Thought it very funny
How could someone of his age[1]
Wager that much money

40

Philip understood their point
But let the bet be done
If only as a lesson
To an all-too-boastful son

41

With terms for the agreement set
The prince began to act
Confidence was never
A quality he lacked

42

The horse feared his own shadow
So he faced him towards the sun
Erasing the problem
He took him for a run

43

The audience was frightened
For the safety of the child
With bated breath they waited
For the animal was wild

44

But Alexander had control
Of this whole situation
Triumphantly returning
To everyone's elation

Philip II witnessing Alexander's taming of Bucephalus as depicted by Doug Jamieson (copyright; used with permission)

45

Now what did Alexander
In his bold uniqueness know
Bucephalus was frightened
Of his very own shadow

46

Everyone was thunderstruck
By this uncanny boy
It's even said the king himself
Stood there and wept for joy

47

Philip sighed amidst his tears
"This realm's too small for you"
Something his precocious son
It seems already knew

48

Alexander loved to learn
He was an avid reader
A hallmark trait for anyone
Destined to be a leader

49

His father was aware of this
And so he scoured the earth
Looking for a learned man
Who'd match his dear son's worth

50

Aristotle fit the bill
Astute in every field
Capable of harvesting
All a mind could yield

Roman copy in marble of a Greek bronze
bust of Aristotle by Lysippos, c. 330 BC

51

He is my second father
Alexander said with a wink
Philip gave me life
That man taught me how to think

52

He learned not to believe
What everyone had said
But test it for himself
And see where all that led

53

This served him well indeed
Whenever facing foes
"How will he attack?" they'd query
Because no one ever knows

54

Strike a balance in all things
His teacher daily taught
But for this unique pupil
That thinking came to naught

55

Excess rather was the key
He liked to roll the dice
Supreme glory was his aim
Regardless of the price

56

The lad would later pay
For ignoring the sage
But he got what he needed
Applause at center stage

PART II — COMING OF AGE

Some years pass
Finding Philip in charge
Of all threats at home
And Europe at large

58

The target was Persia
But before he could go
Philip needed a beachhead
So he sent Attalus and Parmenio

59

While they were off in Asia
Philip communed with the gods
And asked the Delphic Oracle
If he had winning odds

A Roman marble herm with the head of Alexander (Louvre, Paris)

60

"The bull is crowned" he was told
"The consummation is at hand"
"The sacrificer's ready"
Philip didn't understand

61

Over and over he pondered
What it was all about
In the end he gave himself
The benefit of doubt

62

His reading of the prophesy
Deemed himself the sacrificer
Persia then must be the bull
And glory the enticer

63

The king was somewhat blinded
And did not recognize
That the oracle was speaking
Of his very own demise

64

Assuming god's approval
And not remotely fretting
Philip joyously prepared
For his daughter's wedding

65

Her groom another Alexander
The King of Epirus
Uncle to the princess
Through the queen Olympias

66

They flocked from everywhere
To witness this event
Held at ancient Aegae[2]
And gladly they all went

67

Tribute in abundance
To the gods was duly made
But next to Philip's laurels
The rest seemed somewhat staid

68

Philip shone more brightly
With his gifts of golden crowns
Than the gods themselves did
Which brought Olympian frowns

69

You see, both individuals
And city-states alike
Rushed to him with golden crowns
No sign someone would strike

70

Whether by coincidence
Or truly sent by Zeus
Words of darkened destiny
Foretold some stark abuse

71

An actor from Epirus
Was there to give a show
And deride the Persian king
Philip's next great foe

72

"You dream the cultivation
Of the farthest-reaching star
But you are wrong believing
That you'll ever get that far"

73

Philip was intrigued by
The song's prophetic theme
But like the oracle's advice
'Twas not what it might seem

74

Finally with merriment
And reveling all done
The spectators retired
To await the next day's fun

75

So with rosy-fingered Dawn
And Helios leading way
Throngs of Philip's entourage
Began another day

76

The multitude of people
Flocked into the theater
Expecting games and sacrifice
Of frankincense and myrrh

77

Displays of every sort were there
And gift of all that's best
But awe and shock were yet to come
In ways that no one guessed

78

Amidst a great procession
Wrought with artistry and wealth
A grand and mighty warrior
Would lose his life through stealth

79

Other scribes would call it fate
And some a divine grudge
I'll just tell the tale
And let you be the judge

A 3rd-century Roman gold medallion of Philip II
(Bibliothèque nationale de France)

80

Beholding twelve great statues
Each an Olympian god
The people watched as Philip
Chose to make this number odd

81

For alongside the immortals
Majestically enthroned
A likeness of the king himself
Had artfully been honed

82

The king had meant to honor
Both the gods and his position
Never thinking they might
See this as an imposition

83

All the parties waited
For the new god to appear
A fitting climax to
An unsurpassed career

84

He wanted to show all that
He was loved in his land
So the king appeared without
A bodyguard at hand

The assassination of Philip II, depicted in an engraving by 19th-century Italian artist Bartolomeo Pinelli

85

His cloak one minute cloudy white
The next the devil's red
In an instant all was done
The mighty king was dead

86

The man who used his knife
To slash and thrust and rip
Quickly tried to get away
But on a vine he'd trip

87

In any case the killer
Of the king was quickly found
He never had a chance
At once he hit the ground

88

Javelined to death
By a trio of alert men
Pausanias was never
To be seen or heard again

89

The guards had acted swiftly
But killed the boy in haste
He could have told of others
This was a tragic waste

90

The murder of King Philip
Remains a mystery
One of the very greatest
In all of history

91

Was it a lone assassin?
Conspiracy of a few
Was Olympias involved?
And Alexander too?

Onyx cameo of Alexander and Olympias from the 3rd century BC (Historical Art Museum, Vienna)

92

If an answer
Will e'er be found
It lies somewhere in
The murky background

93

Thinking cap on
Just for the fun of it
Let's see how we do
With this tricky whodunit

94

We do know the assassin
Had a personal grief
He was settling a score
And hoping for relief

95

Pausanias was no stranger
To the slaughtered king
He was a royal bodyguard
The two once had a fling

96

Philip was a fickle sort
And it was soon he came
To find another lover
With his former's self-same name

97

Pausanias number one
Did not stop at a frown
He called his young replacement
A hermaphroditic clown

98

The second Pausanias
Couldn't stand the degradation
So he sacrificed himself
To end humiliation

99

Telling his friend Attalus
He couldn't stand the pain
He shielded his old lover
In battle and was slain

100

Now Attalus resented what
Had happened to his friend
And took it on himself
To honor and defend

101

He got the vilifier drunk
In fact he was quite plastered
Then by a score of muleteers
The boy was pederastered

102

Recovered from his stupor
Pausanias number one
Went to Philip promptly
To complain of what was done

103

Although the king had thought
This sordid act lamentable
The question really centered on
Whom he deemed expendable

104

Attalus was the uncle of
King Philip's latest wife
And an able commander
In military life

105

Pausanias was
Merely a bodyguard
Making the choice
Less than hard

106

The king tried to mollify
The bitter boy's emotion
By giving to Pausanias
Some gifts and a promotion

107

Instead he nursed the wrath
Philip failed to appease
And then he sought due counsel
From his tutor Hermocrates

108

Fame was then the topic
Pausanias chose to explore
And the teacher gave a lesson
That was lethal at the core

109

"If you kill the man who's climbed
The ladder of success
As long as he's remembered
They'll remember you no less"

110

No one knows if this man
Had a certain king in mind
But with these words the thoughts
Of regicide aligned

111

There's much more to this story
To eventually unfold
Enter Queen Olympias
The vengeful and the bold

112

Furious and jealous
That Philip took another wife
Some might say irate enough
To shorten Philip's life

113

Nowhere near the scene
When Philip finally died
But rumor said the horses there
Were ones she had supplied

Detail of a Roman gold medallion of Olympias from the 3rd century (Archaeological Museum, Thessalonike)

114

Her actions hinted at
A shared conspiracy
With Philip dead she failed
To mask her sense of glee

115

She honored Pausanias
When once the deed was done
The very man who murdered
The father of her son

116

If this horrific gesture
Had been made by any other
Alexander would have struck her down
But this was his own mother

117

She next dealt with the problem
Of King Philip's widowed bride
By making the young lady
Hang herself in "suicide"

118

And how did this poor woman
Get drawn into her trap?
The Queen had killed her baby
While the child was on her lap

119

Everyone had wondered
What the Queen was up to next
It was with Olympias
That they were rightly vexed

120

From the murder of his father
The prince had much to gain
And recently their kinship
Was under grievous strain

121

So much rancor filled the air
The prince and mother fled
Alexander soon returned
His mother shook her head

122

Attalus was once again
Involved in this dispute
Alexander's claim to power
He elected to refute

123

There had been a scene
At Philip's seventh wedding
Where Attalus had questioned
Alexander's begetting

124

He said he hoped the union
Of King Philip and his bride
Would produce a proper heir
In whom people could take pride

125

Alexander hearing this
Was startled and furious
Hurling his drinking cup
At the man calling him spurious

An ivory carving of Alexander from the 4th century BC (Archaeological Museum, Thessalonike)

126

Attalus then returned in kind
A cup at Philip's son
And this provoked the king
Into action of his own

127

But Philip didn't side
With the man you might expect
He was mad at Alexander
Showing Attalus disrespect

128

A drunken Philip then
Went clearly overboard
Charging at his son
With a drawn and pointed sword

129

Before the king arrived
He had fallen on his face
Causing Alexander
To call him a disgrace

130

"Behold" he said "The man
Who would conquer Asia Minor
And he can't even manage
To walk from his recliner"

131

Some say that Alexander
Wished his father dead
But I don't think he killed him
Just to get ahead

132

Why would any person
Who deeply cherished pride
Kill his own father
And be labeled patricide?

133

However it may well be
He knew ahead of time
About a plot against the king
And ignored it by design

Part III — A Heroic King

The prince received his kingdom
Sooner than was planned
And with it came great tumult
Revolt at every hand

135

For neighboring barbarians
Resented servitude
They longed for their own freedom
And liberties eschewed

136

Equally precarious
Where Greece was concerned
The city-states were well aware
The tables had just turned

The coronation of Alexander depicted in a painting by the French artist Jean Fouquet (Louvre, Paris)

137

Alexander's counselors
Gave him some advice
Appease the warring tribesmen
And to Greece be extra nice

138

Specifically they advised
That he should give up Greece
Ostensibly for harmony
And in the name of peace

139

For bordering barbarians
They gave a quick solution
Placate every rebel tribe
Avoid a revolution

140

Alexander saw all this
As lame passivity
Going both against the grain
And his proclivity

141

He must establish here and now
That he was truly boss
He also had to prove to be
A man you dare not cross

142

And so with his great boldness
Leonine to the core
The king had made it known
The price defiance bore

143

The king of Macedon
Dealt with border foes
With brilliance and ferocity
Striking telling blows

Late-4th-century-BC marble head of Alexander (Museum of Fine Arts, Boston)

144

Next Alexander learned that Thebes
Was conspiring in a plot
Athenians soon sympathized
The king's rage soon ran hot

145

He thus led all his forces
Through the pass Thermopylae
The troops were all elated
With their spirits soaring free

146

They cowered in submission
Athens' fabled fickle city-state
They promised to behave
Or so they said at any rate

147

There was another reason
The king chose to take that route
Demosthenes said something
He simply must refute

148

The orator told Athens
That the king and his whole force
Were massacred up north
An outright lie of course

149

As if this ruse were not enough
To nettle and annoy
When Alexander came to Greece
He called the king a boy

A cast of a portrait statue of Demosthenes (Ashmolean Museum of Art and Archaeology, Oxford)

150

Arriving first at Thebes
Alexander offered to relent
If certain men he named
Were brought shackled to his tent

151

Dismissive in this
Most important matter
It was they who wanted
Hostages and no further chatter

152

Furthermore they urged all Greeks
Who wanted to be free
To join them in their cause
And restore their liberty

153

Alexander felt he had no choice
But to declare a war
His father's power panoply
He needed to restore

154

The Thebans were surrounded
Great numbers fell in battle
Many soldiers heard firsthand
The sound of death's grim rattle

155

The city then was taken
And razed to the ground
Not a trace of habitation
Was left to be found

156

All aspiring heroes
Who escaped their shallow graves
Were herded for an auction
And sold as common slaves

157

Few escaped the sentence
Save those for whom he cared
Priests and friends of Macedon
A poet's kin he spared

158

By destroying Thebes
The king's name invoked fear
If we do what this man wants
He may never come here

159

Thebes and Athens
The two eyes of Hellas
One now plucked out
The other in chaos

160

The lesson was learned
In Athens as well
Appease the young king
Before they too fell

A 3rd-century Roman gold medallion of Alexander (Walters Art Museum, Baltimore)

161

Tell him what he wants to hear
Before it's too late
Do whatever it takes
To avoid Thebes's fate

162

Alexander made his point
In a blood-soaked sack
The Greeks would no longer
Risk his attack

163

Great adventure awaited
Him off in the east
Changing the world
For both man and beast

164

Crossing into Asia
And performing high deeds
He worships the gods
Whose favor he needs

165

First to set foot
Spear in the ground
The claim has been made
And the enemy found

166

Tension abounds
But audacity prevails
The first hurdle's crossed
A new dare he assails

Alexander in the Battle of the Granicus River (334 BC) by the 18th-century Dutch artist Cornelius Troost (Rijksmuseum, Amsterdam)

167

The Lord of Asia
If he's worth his salt
Must solve a problem
Most fail by default

168

The Gordian knot
Remains firmly tied
Even men of great fame
All failed when they tried

169

He ponders the problem
And stares at the knot
Others look on
So fail he cannot

170

The pressure is mounting
Is this task too great?
Must the unconquered hero
Capitulate?

171

He draws his sword
And slashes it through
In one fell swoop
A masterful coup

Alexander and the Gordian knot in a painting by the 18th-century French artist Jean-Simon Berthélemy, ca. 1767

172

Genius is rare
But ordeals abound
And those of his ilk
Want the next to be found

173

Egypt lured our young hero
Gods that beguile
He could not resist
The call of the Nile

The 16th-century German artist Albrecht Altdorfer's painting of the Battle of Issus in 333 BC (Alte Pinakothek, Munich)

174

Welcomed by throngs
A new spirit awoke
Egypt was free
From the Persian yoke

175

He worshipped Apis[3]
In everyone's view
Thus declaring himself
An Egyptian too

Egyptian sphinxes were already more than 2,000 years old by the time of Alexander.

176

Pharaoh now
And a god as well
He'd better beware
Mortal heads swell

177

After founding Alexandria
In Egypt's north
On his hazardous pilgrimage
To Siwah he set forth

A double-snake gold arm bracelet exemplifies the craftsmanship during the reigns of Philip II and Alexander.

178

This trip put the king
In with heroes who
Like Perseus and Heracles
Had gone there too

179

Searing arid sands
Caused the best to refrain
But the young king was blessed
With just enough rain

180

The route was obscured
Sandstorms far and wide
The gods intervened
Two snakes were his guide

181

An oasis at last
And an oracle too
One whose words
Always had been true

182

Ammon was there incarnate
Greeting him as his son
Another great victory
Had already been won

183

He spoke with his "father"
A private affair
Whatever was said
Would ever stay there

Alexander bows before the priest of Ammon (who embodied god) at Siwah (a medieval French miniature).

184

His lineage divine
Alexander was elated
It was time to push on
He rarely ever waited

185

Persian king on the run
His tiara now claimed
Alexander Great King
And none were more famed

Alexander depicted entering Babylon, by 17th-century artist Charles Le Brun (Louvre, Paris)

186

Would Babylon resist
And delay his march east?
A spirited defense
Or a glorious feast?

187

The gates opened wide
And the crowd celebrated
Like subjects in Egypt
At last liberated

188

To many it was
The jewel in the crown
And a fitting climax
For a life of renown

189

To this restless soul
Yes seize these bright days
Good rollicking fun
Then proceed to next phase

Part IV — The Transformation

Ancients were puzzled
By another great mystery
Mentioned by all
Who wrote this man's history

191

How could a leader
With genius and skill
Change for the worse
And plummet downhill?

192

Invincible still
In the face of a foe
He began to see demons
Wherever he'd go

A 1st-century-BC bronze statuette of Alexander astride Bucephalus (National Archaeological Museum, Naples)

193

Friends became suspect
Keep alert for deceivers
Only a handful
Of faithful believers

194

Still they fought on
Victorious in war
Wondering why
He was not like before

195

Some historians now
Have started to think
That perhaps his change
Was connected to drink

196

He drank a lot more
Than other men do
And when he got drunk
The target was you

197

Better be careful
And keep on your toes
Who will be next?
Nobody knows

198

Was he remorseful?
You'd have to say yes
But he did it again
When he drank to excess

199

The fruit of the vine
Had clouded his mind
And things that he did
Were of a strange kind

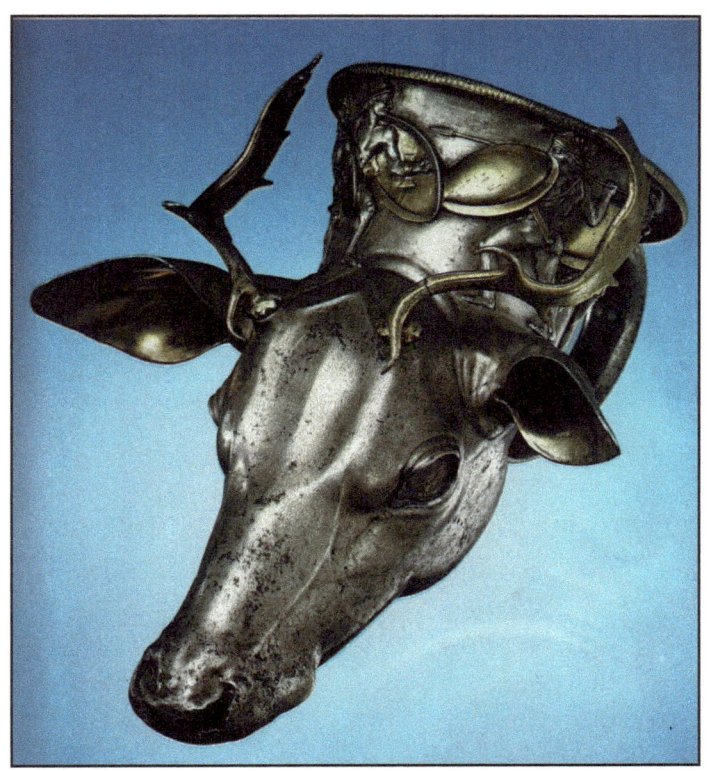

A silver rhyton, or drinking-horn, in the shape of a deer's head; a mythical battle adorns the area surrounding the handle.

200

Just lend your ear
And also your eye
To events that unfold
And then ponder why

Part V — The Ambivalent Victor

P ersepolis could be taken
Without opposition
Its governor provided
Easy acquisition

202

The imperative thing
Was to get there faster
Than the Persian soldiers
And become its master

203

Accordingly the king advanced
Along the rough terrain
Until at once he saw a sight
That filled his soul with pain

204

It was a band of Greeks
Forgotten prisoners of war
All victims of atrocities
The signs of which they bore

205

Mutilated there were no
Noses hands or ears
Most of them had been it seemed
That way for many years

206

The limbs that to their work
Were not directly related
The Persians had decided
To have them amputated

207

These miserable wretches
Asked the king for aid
He said he'd bring them home
But they said no and stayed

208

They reasoned that the Greeks
Would be unduly stunned
At least amongst themselves
They knew they'd not be shunned

A 3rd-century-BC marble head of Alexander (Archaeological Museum, Pella)

209

Agreeing, Alexander then
On recompense decided
Money clothes and food
For each of them provided

210

The king was very kind to them
And made up what he could
For having to experience
What no one ever should

211

He was always empathetic
Towards them considered less
Especially those that others
Were likely to oppress

212

Women too enjoyed
Alexander's grace
Never were mistreated
And warmly were embraced

213

Animals especially
Were treated with great care
It's just human beings
Who better beware

214

They reached Persepolis
And rubbing their eyes
The city they saw
Was the world's greatest prize

215

The king let them pillage
Without any guilt
It was the Persians
For whom it was built

216

His soldiers indulged in
A most vicious sack
They grabbed what they could
In the name of payback

217

The city was stripped
Of its grand majesty
Persepolis now was
A sad travesty

218

Some of the soldiers
Felt an odd twinge
But most were enthralled
By their ransacking binge

219

The king must have thought
Their behavior debased
For him pleasures lay
In the glory he chased

220

Never content
With what he'd attained
Alexander looked forward
To what yet remained

221

The treasure he gathered
Was banked for new wars
Thinking ahead
But time for a pause

222

At a huge banquet
With sacrifices completed
A royal assemblage
Of seventy seated

223

Dionysus god of wine
Was liberally praised
Whenever a cup
Was eagerly raised

224

For after all
The god was in the wine
Drinking brought power
And one felt divine

225

Macedonians were known
To drink to excess
Their fearless young king
Could hoist with the best

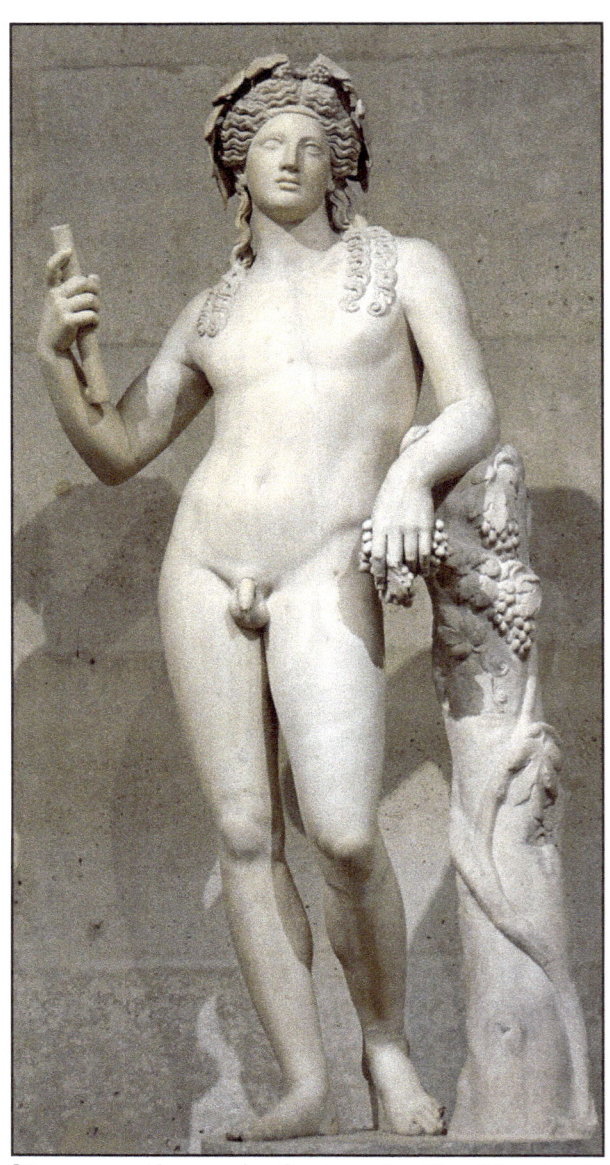
Dionysus, the god of wine, in the Musée du Louvre, Paris (copyright Marie-Lan Nguyen, Wikimedia Commons, CC-BY 2.5; used with permission)

226

Let's just say the affair
Got way out of hand
Alexander and others
More drunk than they'd planned

227

They say a woman
Was initially to blame
Who thought why not set
The palace aflame?

228

Citing King Xerxes
Who torched the Acropolis
Why not repay him
And destroy his metropolis?

229

The act if thought through
Was a real abomination
But for those in their cups
A splendid conflagration

230

"The torches be lit"
Someone said in a burst
But only a king
Is fit to throw first

231

Alexander in a stupor
Was ignited by the notion
Destroying such a palace
What a commotion!

232

Parmenio advised the king
To let the palace be
After all he said
It's now your property

233

Alexander didn't listen
And the palace was a pyre
Once sober he regretted
Setting it on fire

234

Later passing through the ruins
He stopped and shook his head
No doubt quite remorseful
About where his drink had led

235

Parmenio's martial skill
His son did inherit
Philotas rose in the ranks
Through his father and his merit

The ruins at Persepolis

236

His nature was likened
To the very king himself
Valiant and resilient
And a sharer of his wealth

237

But he also put on airs
A bogus majesty
A loftiness of spirit
Unbecoming one as he

238

This streak of self-indulgence
Waxed with battles won
Until his father pleaded
"Pray — be less my son"

239

Philotas was proud and
Oft devoid of grace
Alexander came to look at him
With considerable distaste

240

Looming in the back
Of Alexander's mind
May have been the time
Philotas saw him in a bind

241

He'd stood beside Philip
When the king opened his son's door
And reprimanded Alexander
Like he'd never done before

242

Shame before someone
Is seldom forgotten
And now Philotas was involved
In something misbegotten

243

While he was drinking deeply
At night within his tent
He told tales to his mistress
In confidence meant

244

"Alexander is worth nothing"
said with braggadocio
"Nothing without me
And my father Parmenio"

245

This bedmate of Philotas
Her name was Antigone
Reported what she heard
To the king frequently

246

Alexander chose
To turn the other cheek
For now at least he let
Philotas carry on and speak

247

Ironically the crime for which
He'd pay the ultimate price
Was when he failed to speak
Not once but twice

248

A certain Royal Page
Had learned that his new lover
Was making plans to kill the king
At once he told his brother

249

When brother heard
This startling news
He then told Philotas
There was no time to lose

250

"Philotas, you see Alexander
Each and every day
Tell him of the plot
And do so straightaway"

251

Philotas for whatever reason
Failed to follow his advice
He turned a deaf ear
Not just once but twice

252

An exasperated page
Pleaded to see the king
Once the plot was revealed
It left a bitter sting

253

Alexander forthwith sent
For the boy who launched the plot
But he resisted
And was slain on the spot

254

The king recoiled at the idea
But angrier still
That its leader was dead
Left blanks harder to fill

255

He asked his entourage
For some considered plan
They agreed there was at least
One other guilty man

256

The page they said
Wasn't powerful enough
To orchestrate
Such complex stuff

257

Alexander chose
His council very well
They disliked Parmenio's son
And he had failed to tell

A 4th-century-BC marble head of Alexander (Acropolis Museum, Athens)

258

Soon we find Philotas
Facing the army and on trial
For his role in the plot
He gives a strong denial

259

Alexander makes it
A loyalty test
Whom do you trust?
Who serves you best?

260

Philotas was gone
But his father remained
A legend himself
Brilliant and famed

261

Parmenio was away
With the loyal troops he led
A threat to the king
If he knew Philotas was dead

262

Sealing the camp
To prevent any sort of leak
The king sent a dispatch
With a man he had to seek

263

A friend of Parmenio's
And above reproach
There'd be no apprehension
When he made his approach

The murder of Parmenio depicted in a medieval French miniature

264

As he opened the message
Parmenio was slain
Those who served with him
Inflicting the pain

265

The messenger's family
Was kept by the king
To ensure all went well
And I mean everything

Cleitus behind Alexander at the Battle of the Granicus River (334 BC), where he saved the king's life, depicted in an engraving by the 19th-century Italian artist Bartolomeo Pinelli

266

Another telling lesson
Was learned by all
Never cross the king
Or you're certain to fall

267

Cleitus as well
Met an early demise
This event too was
A stunning surprise

268

His sister nursed Alexander
While he cradled a rattle
Cleitus saved the king's life
At an earlier battle

269

Some friends of the king
Gifted him with fruit
A special occasion
And excuse for a toot

270

The wine flowed freely
A Macedonian's delight
Tall tales were told
And all going right

271

Then a performer
Began his routine
Making fun of the army
For a botched battle scene

272

The old guard resented
Themselves being chided
In the presence of barbarians
They'd been indicted

273

A drunken Cleitus
Shouted how wrong
To hear such drivel
Even in song

274

Cleitus it seems
Was involved in the event
Taking it personally
Fomenting resentment

275

The drunken king
Asked if this misfortune
Wasn't cowardice
Or at least a portion

276

Cleitus sprang to his feet
And to the king loudly said:
"If not for my 'cowardice'
You'd be quite dead"

277

"You're no longer at ease
With your own kind
And we can't even
Speak our own mind"

278

Incensed the king said
"Is this what you exclaim?
Nasty things about your king
Slandering his name?"

279

Alexander threw an apple
Then reached for a knife
To attack the man who
Had brought him such strife

280

An alert bodyguard
Had hidden the dagger
Knowing the king
Was drunk by his stagger

281

Other wise men
Whisked Cleitus away
But sadly the fellow
Returned to the fray

282

He came back boldly
With a defiant lament:
"Alas! What we have
Is evil government"

Alexander kills Cleitus, depicted in an engraving by the 19th-century Italian artist Bartolomeo Pinelli

283

No sooner these words
Did this man spew
Than the king grabbed a spear
And ran Cleitus through

284

After the thrust
He felt deep remorse
Turned the spear on himself
Stopped only by force

285

He spent both night and day
In bitter lamentations
Crying…wailing…keening
Penitential exudations

286

Alarmed at his seclusion
They tried to ease his pain
Futile efforts
Mostly done in vain

287

Then the royal seer
Ascribed it to fate
The king he took notice
And seemed less obdurate

288

They brought in Callisthenes
Historian of the court
But Alexander thought of him
As an insipid sort

289

Another sage though
Thought up a new twist
He risked life and limb
And told the king this

290

"I can't believe Alexander's
Weeping like a slave
Is this how Ammon's son
Is expected to behave?"

291

This sharp talk brought him back
Out of his bereavement
Sadly for Callisthenes
It wasn't his achievement

292

Antiquity describes this man
As not so very wise
From many telling anecdotes
That's easy to surmise

293

Yet it is a trifle harsh
To say that he was dense
More likely Aristotle's nephew
Had no common sense

294

He'd get himself in situations
Where he'd oft offend
The very ones upon whom
This scribe must depend

295

Callisthenes was also billed
As something of a snob
Scarcely a diplomat
With few would he hobnob

296

Alexander liked to be
With men who loved to drink
Not with those like Callisthenes
Who much preferred to think

297

And so the king remembered
When his scribe put up a fuss
Refusing drink lest he would need
The help of Asclepius[4]

298

More on Callisthenes
In just a little while
Meanwhile let's speak of
Women who beguile

299

Love at first sight
They say of Roxane
Was the king smitten
Or was it a plan?

The 16th-century Italian artist Raphael's Alexander and Roxane (Louvre, Paris)

300

He'd waited quite long
And a king has to care
About what will happen
If he sires no heir

301

Hephaestion was beloved
He would die for the man
But produce a child?
That no male can

302

The king had been mired
For two years or more
In Afghanistan
The graveyard of heroes galore

303

Alexander looked east
Towards India and Ocean
And Roxane's father
Let him set plans in motion

304

Now revolts there
Would be handled by him
The prospects were bright
Hitherto they'd been dim

305

Roxane was a blessing
In more ways than one
There were Indian victories
Yet to be won

306

But before new laurels
Could be sought and won
There were problems at court
That must be undone

The marriage of Alexander and Roxane, depicted by 17th-century Italian artist Il Sodoma (Villa Farnesina, Rome)

307

Persians prostrated
Before the Great King
Macedonians did not
And confusion did sting

308

They did this for gods
But not other men
So a change must be made
With real acumen

309

Gradual was the thought
A dress rehearsal
To render the ritual
Less controversial

310

His men would receive
A kiss from the king
As a reward
For their prostrating

311

It was a good plan
But not guaranteed
The king wasn't sure
If his men would accede

312

Most men proved willing
And did so on cue
Callisthenes alone
Did not follow through

313

The king didn't notice
But when told of this
Waved him away
And refused the kiss

A late 4th-century marble head of Alexander
(J. Paul Getty Museum, Malibu)

314

Callisthenes left with
Snide words to save face
Oblivious that he
Had fallen from grace

315

The historian was learned
But the king quick of wit
He waited for a moment
When revenge nicely fit

316

It came at a banquet
Callisthenes orating proud
Reciting the virtues
Of those in the crowd

317

The king said "Of noble subjects
All could speak well
How about our faults
Speak of those pray tell"

318

Callisthenes took the bait
A scorching palinode
Berating all those there
He was certain to goad

319

The king said this speech
Did not prove his skill
Instead it revealed
Mendacious ill will

320

The king's contempt
Had become all too clear
But enveloped in arrogance
The man knew no fear

321

And so when another plot
Of pages was disclosed
Here was the chance
To have him disposed

322

By claiming that Callisthenes
Was intricately involved
Another of the king's problems
Was summarily resolved

323

The vile plot itself
May have come about
Except for Alexander's
All-night drinking bout

324

Several of the pages
Had agreed on a certain night
To slay the king inside his tent
But he was nowhere in sight

325

The chief culprit caught
Pointed to tyranny
As the primary cause
Of their conspiracy

A pitcher from Tomb II at Vergina, created in the 4th-century BC, and the kind of vessel that Alexander used for wines and water at state banquets

326

He harbored a grudge
It's a king he was trashing
Who in front of his peers
Delivered a thrashing

A bronze head of Alexander as part of a nude statue by Lysippos

327

The outcome for Callisthenes
Reminiscent of Philotas
Came from charges
That also seemed bogus

328

Callisthenes was hanged
One source clearly claims
Another thinks death
Came while still in chains

PART VI — INDIA[5]

India beckoned
The king poised to go
A fresh world and horizon
A mighty new foe

330

Across a wide river
The great rajah waits
His elephants putting
The king in bad straits

331

His horses until now
Fearless in a fight
Smelled the huge beasts
And turned in grim fright

332

Alexander tries to cross
Elsewhere and faster
Porus positions his tuskers
Like a seasoned chess master

333

Stymied for longer
Than in all other cases
The king must outsmart
This wise man he faces

334

Watched night and day
Bright light or dim
He picks out a soldier
Who looks just like him

335

Dresses him in royal attire
And across the great waters
There's Alexander —
Emerging from his quarters

336

At night the king goes
With a small force upstream
Crossing the river
Implementing his scheme

A 4th-century-BC coin depicting Alexander attacking mahouts on an elephant

337

This finds the rajah
Confused and perplexed
But his elephants must
Be dealt with next

338

The footmen unseat
Mahouts with their pikes
And strike at the beasts
Where no creature likes

339

They turn in circles
Racked with such pain
Stampeding their own
Just a few remain

340

Alexander triumphs
Against a great foe
A genius on the battlefield
Wherever he'd go

A 4th-century-BC coin depicting Alexander with elephant skins and Ammon's horns (Museum of Fine Arts, Boston)

A tapestry of Alexander and Porus after the Battle of the Hydaspes (Jhelum) River, by the 17th-century French artist, Charles Le Brun (Louvre, Paris)

341

Porus fought nobly
And became an ally
This was a man
Upon whom to rely

342

The king gave his men
A well-deserved rest
Allotting a month
To convalesce

343

The army marched on
Sharing a notion
That they were at last
Quite near to Ocean

344

They fought local tribes
But morale was quite low
Ceaseless rain and the heat
Its own inferno

345

Appalled by conditions
And unbearable weather
The king's men had reached
The end of their tether

346

For eight years now
Away from home
Thousands of miles
They had to roam

347

The king let them pillage
In the hope that gratitude
As in the past would
Alter their attitude

348

But his troops refused
To just let it pass
Insisting they go back
Enough of this morass

349

We won't cross this river
We're turning for home
If you choose to continue
You'll do it alone

350

Compelled to give in
Omens were read
He announced that the gods
Warned — do not forge ahead

351

The troops were elated
But before gathering their things
They had to carry out
An idea of the king's

352

"Just as Heracles had built
Pillars in the west
Let's build huge altars here
To show that we're best"

A silver tetradrachm minted during Alexander's lifetime (photo courtesy of Dorothy Peluso O'Brien)

353

Twelve altars in all
Went up beside the river's shore
Artfully structured
Sturdy not poor

354

He had colossal chairs
Strewn in the right place
So posterity would say
A mammoth race!

355

They headed south
The long route back home
Plenty more bloodshed
Wherever they roam

Part VII — Death in Babylon

Finally back at Susa
Where the king would organize
And bestow some honors
On those who'd earned a prize

357

He learned from watching Philip
That a timely marriage bond
Within the body politic
Was like a magic wand

358

Looking ahead to
How this would end
He decided it best
To create a mixed blend

359

So he married off
Eighty of his most elite
To the noblest Persian girls
A startling feat

360

He held a splendid feast
For those already wed
A total of nine thousand guests
All generously fed

361

Alexander gave each groom
A golden wedding cup
Announcing that all debts accrued
He is picking up

362

A global vision on his part
Europe and Asia as one?
Or simply vested interest
Now that he had won

363

The children of these unions
Would be under his command
To him they would be loyal
Not to any race or land

An 8th-century Coptic textile of Alexander on horseback (Textile Museum, Washington, DC)

364

No matter how glorious
His life had become
The refrain of more
Would beat like a drum

365

His father's ghost
Loomed large in his mind
Competing with him
More knots to unwind

366

Philip was almost
A god while still living
Outdo him again
With no misgiving

367

Ask the Greeks first
They'll likely comply
Becoming a god
You need not die

368

The Greeks acquiesced
To avoid his abuse
In fact they'd agree
If he wished to be Zeus

369

To them it was yet
Another clear sign
Of sheer delusion
And personal decline

370

Somber events
Would soon arise
Portents that foreshadowed
Imminent demise

Marble head of Hephaestion, 4th century BC
(J. Paul Getty Museum, Malibu)

371

Hephaestion's death and
The king's shared a link
The common denominator
For both was drink

372

Hephaestion fell ill
And despite a grim warning
Drank half a gallon of wine
Early in the morning

373

The king rushed to his side
Alas it was too late
The fruit of the vine had
Sealed his fate

374

Alexander mourned
Like no one ever before
Beside himself in grief
He made it clear…and more

375

The doctor was the first to die
For negligence acute
Alexander settling
His own malpractice suit

376

He wreaked havoc on
A local tribe as well
Massacring boys to men
Under anger's spell

377

Hephaestion was gone
It was lonely at the top
But Alexander never knew
When it was time to stop

378

Driven by a force
Only he could understand
The king compelled to carry on
To yet another land

379

First return to Babylon
That was what he thought
For without proper planning
This idea would come to naught

380

Omens and soothsayers
Warned him to beware
This seductive city
Could be a lethal lair

381

Alexander entered
With fear and trepidation
Perhaps his hubris invited
Divine retaliation

382

And so to shield himself
From any celestial malice
Sacrificers flatterers diviners
All came to fill his palace

Alexander as Mars (Louvre, Paris)

383

He took to sacrificing
As a means of escape
While drowning all his misery
Inside the potent grape

384

Alexander craved
A dulling of the senses
Even though it drained
His body of defenses

385

When fever struck
Physicians held their tongue
A wrong diagnosis and
And that was their swan song

386

With parched palate
He demanded more wine
Not just merely water
Liquid fire from the vine

387

Gulping it down
At an inhuman pace
As if he were running
That one final race

Alexander's death depicted in a 4th-century Persian miniature

388

First delirium
And then cold death
The king lay there
Without a breath

389

It was hard to believe
But all could see
He was gone at thirty-two
Three twenty-three BC

A painting, presumed to be of Alexander, by 17th-century Dutch artist Rembrandt

390

Unthinkably grand
In all that he did
Regrettably sad
In all that he hid

A Select Bibliography

Bosworth, A.B. Conquest and Empire: The Reign of Alexander the Great (Cambridge, 1988)
Briant, P. Alexandre le Grand (Paris, 1974)
Carney, E. Olympias (New York, 2006)
Cartledge, P. Alexander the Great: The Hunt for a New Past (New York, 2004)
Freeman, P. Alexander the Great (New York, 2011)
Goldsworthy, A. Philip and Alexander: Kings and Conquerors (New York, 2020)
Green, P. Alexander of Macedon 356-323 BC (Berkeley and Oxford, 1991)
Hamilton, J.R. Alexander the Great (Pittsburgh, 1982)
Hammond, N.G.L. Alexander the Great, King, Commander, and Statesman (Park Ridge, N.J. 1994)
Lane Fox, R. Alexander the Great (New York, 2004)
Naiden, F.S. Soldier, Priest, and God: A Life of Alexander the Great (Oxford, 2019)
O'Brien, J.M. Alexander the Great: The Invisible Enemy. A Biography (London, 1992)
Renault, M. The Nature of Alexander (New York, 1976)
Schachermeyr, F. Alexander der Grosse: Das Problem seiner Persönlichkeit und seines Wirkens (Vienna, 1973)
Thomas, Carol G. Alexander the Great in His World (Oxford, 2007)
Will, W. Alexander der Grosse (Stuttgart, 1986)
Worthington, I. By the Spear: Philip II, Alexander the Great, and the Rise and Fall of the Macedonian Empire (Oxford, 2014)

TABLE OF DATES

Date BC	Stanza	Event or Person and Line from Stanza
7/20/356	1	The Birth of Alexander "Twenty days into July"
382-336	2	Philip II "His father's name was Philip"
c. 375-316	2	Olympias "His mother was Olympias"
d. 326	32	Bucephalus "Bucephalus was a restless sort"
384-322	50	Aristotle "Aristotle fit the bill"
c. 390-336	58	Attalus "So he sent Attalus and Parmenio"
c. 400-330	58	Parmenio "So he sent Attalus and Parmenio"
c. 355-308	64	Philip's daughter Cleopatra "For his daughter's wedding
c. 371-331	65	Alexander of Epirus "The King of Epirus"
d. 336	95	The assassin Pausanias "Pausanias was no stranger"
c. 336	107	Hermocrates "From his tutor Hermocrates"
384-322	147	Demosthenes "Demosthenes said something"
335	155	Thebes Destroyed "And razed to the ground"
334	165	Asia Minor "First to set foot"
333	168	The Gordian knot "The Gordian knot"
331	177	Alexandria "After founding Alexandria"
331	181	Oracle at Siwah "An oasis at last"
331	187	Babylon "The gates opened wide"

(Continued on next page)

330	214	Persepolis "They reached Persepolis"
c. 518-465	228	Persian King Xerxes "Citing King Xerxes"
?362-330	235	Philotas "Philotas high in the ranks"
375-328	267	Cleitus "Cleitus as well met an early demise"
360-c. 327	288	Callisthenes "They brought in Callisthenes"
d. 310	299	Roxane "Love at first sight"
356-324	301	Hephaestion "Hephaestion was beloved"
326	330	Battle of the Hydaspes (Jhelum) River "Across a wide river"
c. 326	332	Porus "Porus posit ons his tuskers"
326	349	"Mutiny" Hyphasis (Beas) River "We won't cross the river"
324	359	The Susa Marriages "So he married off"
324	368	Alexander's Deification "The Greeks acquiesced"
6/10/323	390	The Death of Alexander "In all that he hid"

Endnotes

1. His age was probably between 9 and 12.

2. This was the ancestral Macedonian capital.

3. Their sacred bull.

4. The medical god.

5. To some ancient Greeks, India began across the Hindu Kush mountain range in modern Pakistan, while to others it was the land east of the Indus River.

About the Authors

CHRISTINE O'BRIEN holds an honors degree in classical civilization from Boston College. She has hitherto been working with disabled and elderly people, and this epic poem constitutes her literary debut.

JOHN MAXWELL O'BRIEN is an emeritus professor of history at Queens College (CUNY). His best-selling biography, ALEXANDER THE GREAT: THE INVISIBLE ENEMY, has been translated into Greek and Italian. He has published numerous articles on ancient and medieval history as well as the history of alcoholism, and is the author of "Alcoholism" in the OXFORD CLASSICAL DICTIONARY. Professor O'Brien has also published several dozen poems in literary journals, and his celebrated novel, ALOYSIUS THE GREAT, revolves around a drunken history professor writing a biography of Alexander.

www.ingramcontent.com/pod-product-compliance
Lightning Source LLC
Chambersburg PA
CBHW061209070526
44583CB00025B/3181